THE WORLD ACCORDING TO Walinets

Stan Walinets' four line poems as published in
The Northern Echo 1997 - 2004

First published July 2004 by IRON Press
5 Marden Tce, Cullercoats, North Shields, Northumberland
England, NE30 4PD
Tel/Fax: +44 (0) 191 253 1901
Email: seaboy@freenetname.co.uk
website: www.ironpress.co.uk
ISBN 0 906228 99 9

© Stan Walinets 2004
Typeset in Times New Roman

Pagesetting and layout by Kate Jones
Printed by Tyneside Free Press, Charlotte Square, Newcastle upon Tyne

IRON Press is a member of Independent Northern Publishers

IRON Press books are distributed by Central Books
and represented by
Inpress Ltd, 1st Floor
52 Harpur St, Bedford
MK40 2QT
Tel: +44 (0)1234 330023
Fax: +44 (0) 1234 330024
Email: jon@inpressbooks co.uk
Web: www.inpressbooks.co.uk

Introduction

Newspapers and poetry don't make natural bedfellows. Few poetry books are reviewed in papers, and even less modern poetry is actually published in the press. The daily poem from *The Independent* was a splendid exception, but against that are the countless *Poetry Corner* sections in newspapers which indulge the doggerel sent in by readers. So the partnership between Stan Walinets and *The Northern Echo* is to be congratulated. Thus far it has lasted eight years, and shows little sign of flagging. Stan's weekly Four-Liner is always a model of brevity and concise observation; his eye may fix itself on the dangers of global warming, or the impossibility of finding your way round the Tyneside Metro Centre, the hypocrisy of Christmas, or the crisis in the Balkans. It is almost always amusing but also often deadly serious. IRON Press is delighted to bring out this selection. It's maybe significant that Stan's Four-Liners, like the popular form, the haiku (which IRON Press also publishes and encourages) carries little of the baggage that makes people often so suspicious of much modern poetry. There is no obfuscation, there are no riddles or deeply obscured messages. There is a powerful clarity, plus an instinct for poetry to engage itself in public matters of the day that has a long and radical tradition in British verse. Each poem is of its time, but the collection evokes a whole span of recent history in a way that no normal documentary could.

Peter Mortimer - *Editor, IRON Press*

STAN WALINETS enjoyed a variety of occupations after leaving Leeds Technical School in 1948. He was a time-served watchmaker, half-skilled garage mechanic, van driver, RAF National Serviceman, shop assistant, Father Christmas for a season in Harrods (Prince Charles aged seven was a customer…), and so on, until working in childrens' homes led to training at LSE as a Probation Officer. Marriage, three fine sons and a varied career in social work followed, punctuated by writings in professional journals which on occasion successfully challenged legal mind-sets in the delinquency field. He now lives retired in lovely Teesdale, writing busily – his *100 Mickleton Years* (1994) raised several thousand pounds for Mickleton's new Village Hall. When not writing, he may be seen zooming through the dale

The Years

7
1997

15
1998

27
1999

51
2000

39
2001

65
2002

79
2003

93
2004

1997

Labour Government with massive majority after "Thatcher Years"... Mrs T creates The Thatcher Foundation at taxpayer's expense (currently £60,000 a year and rising)... 'New Labour' gets down to either reversing the damage of those years; or to building on Mrs Thatcher's achievements, depending on which side of the fence you're sitting... The rest of us set about digesting the substantially changed life and life-styles the Thatcher years created for us... Another Lady also visibly affects the nation's life, by her widely mourned death...

Here's the story of
Motorway Fred
First he felt drowsy
Then he was dead

Is it a movie? Is it a tape?
Is it a video? Chat-show?
Goodness me - look -
It's a book!

Fans filling terraces
Cheer up the lads
But fans glued to telly screens
Watch more ads

❖

On ye olde village green
Played ye old cricket team
Now they're a Squad.
How odd.

June 23 (3 rhymes launched the series), July 7

Grandad got sacked
Dad got redunded
I got downsized
We all got defunded

❖

NEEB got sold off
To t' North Electric shower
North Electric flogged it off
Now it's Yankee Power

❖

Abandon hope
All ye who enter
Map-less
Into the Metro Centre.

❖

Away with the Monarchy!
A President let there be!
Now - who'll the people vote for?
Oh Gawd - it's Lady T!

July 14, 21, 28, August 4

Mammoth Sale!
Pay Nothing Now!
Catch you later
And how...

'Standard'; 'Medium';
'Premium'; et cetera
Different words instead of 'small'
Make 'small' look bettera.

When we were young the toothpaste
Did as it was told
But now each time we roll it up
The wretched tube unfolds

The Gents of the Press
Pressed
And Di
Died

August 11, 18, 25, September 1

My hold-all's an ad for Adidas.
His cap badge sells Newcastle beer.
Her T-shirt's a hoarding for Gucci.
We *pay* to display these? How queer!

When caught with an urge
you might use the soft verge
But if you'd grow older
avoid the hard shoulder

In days gone by
Man was the Hunter
Now
He's a punter

❖

An angry young couchee said "Freud –
"I think all your theories are veud!"
"U-huh?" said the sage, noting his rage,
"Zen vhy are you *qvite* so anneud?"

September 8, 15, 22, 29

For darkness, dirt
And desolation
Visit Darlington
Bus Station

Brighton, Eastbourne, Blackpool and
Claims of clear blue water
Now it's back to Westminster
and doing what they oughter

Cassini-load of plutonium blasted into space
Polluted genes of soya beans in your face
"I'm bigger than you are, so I can!"
Says Uncle Sam

Umpteen billion dollars
That's quite a lot
For Defence
From what?

October 6, 13, 20, 27

Digital! Satellite!
Terrestrial! Cable!
We consumers must have CHOICE!
Advertisers' fable?

❖

Car makers boast
of their 0-60 figure
Child deaths rise
with associated vigour

❖

Says evil Saddam, Middle East blight,
"Yank spies, get off my soil!"
But Yanks stand firm for Human Rights
(for 'Human Rights', read 'oil')

❖

Sex sells soap!
Sells cars in a trice!
But we mustn't sell sex
That's not nice

November 3, 10, 17, 24

"We don't need permission to keep our emissions,"
says Old Sam, "So go boil your head.
We don't give a damn about ozone-layer holes
We'll make out with loop-holes instead."

"What use is Christmas,"
kiddies fret,
"If what you see
ain't what you get?"

December 15, 22

1998

Far East economies collapse – but Big Brother Corporations still rule the world... Saddam Hussein gives headaches to the UN... Labour gets into its stride; sometimes tripped up by the likes of Rupert Murdoch... N. Ireland Agreement reached, while everyone goes on disagreeing... Monsanto creep GM crops further into UK... Milosevic still up to nasty tricks... General Pinochet comes to England and gets arrested – Lady Thatcher tries to bail him out... President Yeltsin rules Russia ... MI5 caught out for past surveillance of subversives – such as Jack Straw, now Home Secretary... New drug helps men stand up for themselves... Will we, won't we, join the Euro...?

It's 1998!
May pardons flow from Heaven
For all who wrote the date today
as 5/1/97

❖

When Russia collapsed -
"COMMUNISM FAILED!"
Now the Tiger's tottering -
"CAPITALISM NAILED!"

❖

Spare a thought for America
Pitiful to see
"We need protection from CUBA!"
Oh dear me

❖

He stores vast stocks of gas and germs
That's what Saddam does
We know for sure he's got them
He bought them from us

January 5, 12, 19, February 16

The World might thrive
With international co-operation
But what we have is
Multinational Corporations

❖

Was it plain politics
That worked against Connery,
Or saying 'Slap women!'
That made him less Honnery?

❖

Dear Ramblers, you won't need laws,
The Landowners aren't fools
Of *course* they'll play the game with you
They just want to make the rules

❖

Knee jerk prejudice
Homespun hocus pocus
Tend to be the product
Of Groups labelled Focus

Pity that the fun
of copulation
Too often ends in
Population

The loyal fan supports his Team
But really, he's a learner
The Boardroom chaps just see him as
A nice little earner

Labour dares not, can not rule
And democracy becomes a mockery
For in the end we most of us vote
In line with the whims of Murdochery

Irish Agreement
Gives Peace a chance
But zealots in the spotlight
Will stick to their dance

March 23, 30, April 13, 20

Of all the vacuous
Things to say
Can you beat
'Have a nice day!' ?

❖

When we've frittered away Earth's resources
And life becomes too hard to bear
Don't fret! They've found water deep in the Moon
So NASA will ship us out there.

❖

Welcome, honoured Emperor
Please, not to worry
But one word you should really learn is
Sorry.

❖

Plastic cup 'n' cutlery
Polystyrene plate
That's what makes McDonalds
Absolutely grate

April 27, May 11, June 1, 8

Driving in Spain?
Brill.
But watch the bloody Guardia
Civil

❖

Prior to Slobodan Milosevic
Jugoslavia was span and spic
O come back, Marshall Tito
It's time Slob got the veto

❖

Old Monsanto wants your farm
Ee-i-ee-i-o
So ditch all that E-col-o-gy
He'll tell you what to grow

❖

Marching, drumming, piping
To vex folk in Garvaghy
Is Christian and Principled?
Don't give me that malarghy!

June 15, 22, 29, July 6

We know that life
Is full of care
But isn't all this football
Just that bit too much to bear?

❖

Among the many benefits
Of men taking Viagra
We might well find
There's much less macho aggra

❖

We criticise 'the bureaucrats'
For spending public money
But when the service grinds to a halt
That's 'bureaucrats' too. Funny...

❖

Oh Mr Straw
What shall we do?
I think MI5's watching me
And I bet they're still watching you

July 13, 20, August 10, 17

To avoid the young thinking me crass
I pronounce the word 'bass'
As 'base'
Just in cass

Since the Russians elected Yeltsin
They've done nothing but tighten their beltsin
If they'd stuck with Gorbachev
They might have been betterev

With Man U fans we all cry "Foul!
That Murdoch - he ain't got no soul!"
But didn't we realise, poor fishes
When first we got hooked on his dishes?

Forty million pounds and six years' work
On a sex investigation
America leads the world
In job creation

August 24, September 7, 14, 21

We don't need the Royals any more
They can leave, for all we care.
"Queen's Head To Go From Ecu Notes"
Hey – Brussels – don't you *dare*!

❖

"I'll pop out and murder some villagers,"
Says Slob, "before I cop tea.
The UN will grumble and bumble
But I know they'll do nothing to stop me."

❖

Mary had a little lamb
£2, the Auction bid
Now it's in the Supermart
At 4oz to the quid

❖

In one-to-one
Business gets done
But one-on-one
Sounds fun

September 28, October 5, 12, 19

"Hey guys – keep shtum
'bout Pinochet –
We gave him the job!"
Says the CIA

❖

Blow, blow, thou Winter's wind
Floods, storms - we've really sinned
Too late now to say a prayer
And hope He'll plug the ozone layer

❖

The private lives of public folk
We're told, are always news
But oddly, we never see Editors
Paraded in the World of the Screws

❖

Northumbrian Water is owned by the French…
Northern Electric's the Yanks…
Monsanto's controlling the food that we eat…
The buggers don't even say "Thanks"

October 26, November 2, 9, 23

Pro-Pinochets say "Sure, he tortured
But he's old now, let him go
'Cos shouldn't what's past be forgotten?"
Well…. No

Through years in Opposition
Tony carved his covenant
But miracles get difficult
In Government

"I told Pinochet I would fix it
As sure as I rule Brobdingnag
But wretched Straw now disobeys me.
How *dare* he? Where's my handbag?"

❖

In the tiniest of islands,
Peninsulas and isthmuses,
Folks is wishing other folks
The happiest of Christhmusses

November 30, December 7, 14, 21

So that's another Christmas passed
Did you find it pleasant?
Oh sure, except I'm now in hock
To the ghost of Christmas presents

December 28

1999

Weird weather - flu epidemic cripples NHS; 5,000 people dead in Venezuelan floods... Total eclipse of the Sun... Macpherson Report on 1993 Stephen Lawrence murder - racism clearly involved... France bans British beef... Scotland and Wales achieve home rule...ish... WTO meets in Seattle and London, to riotous welcome... Serbs 'clean' Albanians out of Kosovo, NATO obliged to bomb sense into everyone... Prince Edward engaged to Sophie Rhys-Jones... Robin Cook engages with 6 other ladies... Clinton engages with Monica... Yeltsin disengages whole Government... Aitken and Archer in perjury...

There's a split! There's a row!
Everyone in Government's doing it now!
At least, that's what the media feedya
"No time for *facts* – I'm a *journalist! Pow!*"

❖

"Make your goods cheaper!"
"We're Consumers!" *We* told 'em!
Till the factory went bust.
And the workers? We doled 'em…

❖

Robin Cook had *six* affaires
Disgusting! Alley cat!
They ought to kick him out
I'm glad *I'm* not like that

❖

Answer – Yes! or No!
Don't want your ha's and hum's please
This is Today!
And *I'm* John Humphreys!

January 4, 11, 18, 25

Supermarts *and* corner shops
All £90 a year?
This new Food Standards Agency
Has daft ideas of 'fair'.

❖

Explaining world events
Is hard work for media gents
Whereas Hoddle
Was a doddle

❖

In the name of 'recycling'
Brussels boosts car-makers' wealth
By closing all the scrapyards
So I can't do it myself

❖

Indian peasants? Organic Brits?
Governments? What the hey!
We rule the world.
We're Monsanto. You just pay.

February 1, 8, 15, 22

It took a black lad's murder
While he waited for a bus
To show how racist folk can be –
others, of course. Not us.

Kindly don't tell me to
'Have a nice day!'
Unless you can fix it
To happen. OK?

When Hitler marched on the Czechs
Chamberlain said 'Let's forget it…'
Now Slobodon's torching out villagers
Do we do nowt – and live to regret it?

If deep down you feel a failure,
A no-good. A scruff.
Find a crowd. Then throw a nail bomb.
That'll show you're *tough*

March 1, 8, 29, May 3

Kosovo's now a ruin
And mostly it's our doin'
But Slob ain't gonna cry *'Nuff!*
... so ... let's call the whole thing off

Whether the weather
Is fair or foul
Why is it teenagers
Always seem to scowl?

Consumerism is bad.
We should be stopping.
Trouble is
I do like shopping

Hurray! Bank Holiday Monday!
Relax! Let's frolic and caper!
Except of course the poor guys
Who worked all night on this paper

May 10, 17, 24, 31

At the Euro Elections
We'd probably have voted
But the Press said we wouldn't
So we didn't

They swore they'd present to the Nation
Freedom of Information!
"Oh I know it was *promised*" says Straw
… but that was *before*…"

Turns out the brutal Pinochet
Was aided way back by the CIA.
Not for us, such a key revelation
'Cos Straw rules *our* "Freedom" of Information

"I'll donate you my heart, "said the corpse
"'Cos clearly I won't want it back –
"But tell me, dear patient, will you refuse
"if the doctor tells you I'm black?"

June 21, 28, July 5, 12

Can't see myself in cyberspace
'midst E-mails, /webs and //internets
Wish they'd let me be
just ... *Walinets*

❖

If disordered personality is a crime
Shall we lock up everyone who shows the signs?
Like politicos who lead us into war?
Or even that strange fellow Mr Straw?

❖

Unless I can get in a
Supply of pin-holed cardboard to protect my retina,
Seems this eclipse of the Sun
Ain't gonna be fun

❖

An animal torn to pieces
Is Nature, when all's said and done
But what I can't stand is fox hunters
Who do it for fun

July 19, 26, August 9, 16

The makers of animal drugs
In order to comfort us mugs
Have named the trade body which furthers their wealth
"The National Office of Animal Health"

❖

When the Neighbours cast wraps for the day
And the cameras cease to roam
Do grown-ups drive up in their cars
To take all those teenagers home?

❖

You will work hard for your GCSEs
You will study in our nice white blouses
You will be a model pupil and make us proud
But no dear, you may *not* wear trousers

❖

"Don't march in to save East Timor –
"If you do", says Habibie, "You'll rue it
"We've plenty of arms to fight you –
"You sold 'em to us, we can do it!"

August 23, 30, September 6, 13

I'm a TV News man
So when I quiz a Minister
All I want to do
Is make him look sinister

❖

I have to say
That annual Party Conferences
Are really merely Rallies
And should be called Nonferences

❖

'Gracious thanks,' says Gen. Pinochet
'For your help, dear Lady T –
'I know if you'd the power
'You'd be evil, just like me'

❖

Are the French, in refusing
l'Anglaise boeuf
Just twisting the rules
For all they're woeuf?

September 20, October 4, 11, 18

Disgusting! Sex! On Channel 4!
O let mine eyes not dwell!
And yet – my parents did it...
Well well.

On and on goes the brawl over beef
Did ever you hear such a row?
Myself, I can't see what the fuss is about
But then – I'm only a cow

Down 't fact'ry we work wi' great skill
Mekkin weapons, for export, to kill
We all know we shouldn't but still ...
if *we* don't... someone else will ...

Private health insurance
Takes pressure off the NHS!
But who pays to train their doctors?
Guess

October 25, November 1, 8, 15

Cherie is having a baby
and the dynasty boasts a new scion
Politics being the game it is
Shall we soon hear from Ffion?

❖

What shall it profit Man to free World Trade
If he destroy the Earth?
So watch WTO and Big Business
For all you're worth

❖

From January, no more pounds 'n' ounces
On the scales of your local corner grocer
It's grams 'n' kilos, else the Council pounces…
Won't the EC change its mind? No sir!

❖

O Lord, please forgive us
For I guess we *must* have sinned
Otherwise, why hast Thou sent
This endless rain and howling bl**dy wind?

November 20, 29, December 6, 13

My approval of the Media
I have now rescinded
Since the bulk of them decided
"Let's get Prescott winded!"

'Tis the season of goodwill
Yet friends stare at me… hard…
Oh Lordy! I forgot
to send a Christmas Card

December 20, 27

2000

The new Millennium dawns, the World doesn't end... We sell Hawks to Nigeria – purely for defence (!)... Monsanto changes its name... Home Sec lets General Pinochet go back home... £800 million new building for GCHQ... Couple fined for snogging on a 'plane... Plan to pay pensioners through banks – 1000 small POs close... Euan Blair has a holiday... David Shayler exposes MI5 & MI6 as law-breakers... New Act gives asylum seekers food vouchers instead of cash... Ann Widdicombe promises zero tolerance for cannabis ... Autumn flood disasters... Rail crashes at Hatfield & Paddington... New US President 'elected' by hanging chads...

Tyson comes in? Pinochet goes free?
And juries might soon cease to try you and me?
"Oh believe it, stop whingeing," says Straw
"*I'm* the Law!"

So we'll sell more Hawks to Nigeria?
We..e..ll ... they'll only kill a *few* more kids...
I know it's not an *Ethical* Policy
But y'see, we've had higher bids...

It's a crime to 'promote' what some people don't like
Ordains Section 28
Yet celibate churchmen think they've the right
To promote how *they* think we should mate

Monsanto
Who failed to sell us GM food
Have changed their name, to Pharmacopia.
Don't ask why. That would be rude

January 17, 24, 31, February 7

A Childrens Home? But our estate's exclusive!
If they're in care, they're *bound* to be abusive
Kindly put them elsewhere, we entreat
For instance – can't they just sleep on the street?

❖

Our snap-shut double-brush hi-tech letter box
Will keep out anything the elements might bring us
Except that our front door echoes with frequent knocks
From Postmen shouting "Ouch! My bloody fingers!"

❖

Poor Mr Pinochet
So ill that Justice just can't have its say
And even back home in Chile
He'll *never* get well again – will he?

❖

They're spending £800 million
To build a new GCHQ
The better to bug all our enemies
And also to bug me and you

February 21, 28, March 6, 13

The Rover's a very fine car
But fashion dictates that it's borin'
In consequence, slaves that we are,
We're naff if our car isn't foreign

Repeal Section 28?
That is *not* the people's choice!
I'm Baroness Young
So *I* am the people's voice

"The bottom line," he said,
"At the end of the day,
"Is the innovation uptake.
"What more can I say?"

Did you hear about that couple
Fined for snogging on that 'plane?
Disgusting, when we all know
That we'd love to do the same

March 20, 27, April 3, 10

"*Mu-u-m* ... I *need* just one more Pokemon pack
Then I can win us all that money back
Y'see, it *might* just have the rarest card…
Come *on* Mum … £2.60 … don't be hard…"

❖

Seven Cabinet Ministers all come from this Region
The implications are truly legion
Now that jobs in coal and steel have all but ceased
Is Ministering the 'in' job, in the new North East?

❖

Don't look down your nose at my motor
Like, nudge-nudge and rather amused
It's *not* second-hand, I'd have you know –
It's *pre-used*

❖

Tone *wants* to re-distribute wealth
But fears he must do it by stealth
Which then means that nobody knows
So the faithful get cross and oppose

April 24, May 1, 8, 15

Folk who've actually been there say
They loved it, when they get back home
But all the little journalists love to play
"Let's All Knock The Dome!"

Paisley's Democratic Unionists
Will re-join the Irish Assembly
But what *they* mean by 'democracy'
Rather reminds me of Wembley

No-one minds or calls it rude
When we enjoy our human need for food
But when we feel our human need for sex –
'Goodness me!' folk cry, 'Whatever next?'

Say what you like about Europe
For my part I hope it succeeds
It's *got* to be better than leaving world rule
To the madmen America breeds

May 29, June 5, 19, 26

Show me the way to genome
I'm tired and I want to go to bed
I'll wait till they can clone me up a few new parts
That's the future way to get ahead

❖

Twinkle twinkle little chip
How you have us in your grip
Glued to the screen, stuck in the house
Am I a man or am I a mouse?

❖

Good news from Gordon Brown –
spoiled by leaks. What fun!
So shall we still vote Labour?
Or should we elect the Sun?

❖

Some bloke we met thought he'd heard a rumour
That this guy was a paedophile
So we strung him from a lamp post.
Community spirit. That's our style

July 3, 17, 24, 31

The way he treats people he meets on 'Today' –
so rude, like their words aren't worth tuppence
So it's rather good news to hear that at last
John Humphrys has had his comeuppance

I, sir, am the Editor of 'News of the World'
And mob-law's not my purpose, I must stress
But why *shouldn't* vigilantes kill who they please?
It's good for – No, you *can't* have my address

Global warming is fact. This next 100 years
Will see our kids freeze, and theirs die of thirst
It's now plain to see that we must fear the worst
So we *must* give up motors. Let's *do* it... You first...

We'll trace you here
We'll click you there
You can't just have a holiday
You're Euan Blair

August 7, 14, 21, 28

They're great at chasing footballs
And ace at making noise
But when it comes to brainwork
We'd best choose girls, not boys

Democracy rules in the US of A!
They can vote any Joe to be President
Provided that Joe can beg enough bucks
From corporate business residents

"Laws? Forget 'em! *We* do as we like!"
Sneered MI5 and MI6 –
So bully for Shayler who got on his bike
And wised us up to their dirty tricks

❖

Don't you hate what
Some Israelis do
To Arabs? I do.
And I'm a Jew

September 4, 11, 18, October 16

"I *insist* that we privatise railways"
Prime Minister Thatcher said
Just think – if she'd been on that Hatfield train
She might now be ….

With rail and health and suchlike
The unavoidable facts is
You wanna decent service?
You gotta pay your taxes

Happily watching truck drivers blockade
Laying blame for their fuel costs on tax,
The oil firms push prices up even more
Quite un-noticed, on truck drivers' backs

Across the world
There's a terrified hush
At the thought of a White House
Under brain-challenged Bush

October 23, 30, November 6, 13

"Good morning!" she said, "We value your call!
"This is BigSales, the Store for Today!
"My name is Sharon. How can I help?"
I hung up. Forgot what I'd wanted to say.

❖

Ten years back, Thatcher got the push.
Know what she left, on our back burner?
A new little law, by which for evermore
We pay her nearly £60-thou a year. Nice little earner…

❖

Trimming my toenails, nicked my skin,
Whatever shall I do?
Scissors shop didn't warn me of that risk …
Think I'll sue…

❖

Media words for sex today
Are all rather in yer face
Time was when News of the World would say
"Intimacy took place…"

November 20, 27, December 4, 11

Bush, campaigning, was famed for his gaffs –
Boobs and howlers, quite without precedent
So how will he now solve world problems?
"Don' ask *me*, I'm only da President…"

December 18

2 0 0 1

BSE banished – then Foot and Mouth... Mass sheep slaughters, farmers ruined (&compensated).. tourist businesses ruined (tough)... Labour landslide... Hague resigns... Mandelson accused of lying... Voter throws egg at Prescott ... UK spy-plane crashes in China...Kurds flee Saddam – Home Office sends them back... Ronnie Biggs surrenders in a wheelchair... Sharon batters Palestine refugee camps... Jamie Bulger murder ... IRA decommissions... September 11 ... bin Laden crowned World Bogeyman... Afghanistan flattened... Bush & Blunkett crack down on everyone... Christmas Day in the USA – a Virgin(ia) birth – piglets cloned...

Spent up and in debt, all on things we don't need
Time we wised up – let's get drastic
Consumers of the world, unite!
You've nothing to lose but your plastic!

Just 'cos I'm rich don't mean I *must* be greedy.
And gifts from me are therefore seedy.
I want to see that Labour wins the fight.
So my money goes where my mouth is, alright?

U.S. TO BASE STAR WARS IN NORTH YORKS?
Our Tony'll probably let 'em
Then states aiming nukes at Uncle Sam
– you've guessed it – it's us who'll get 'em!

I'm gonna demand a refund
It's the biggest dot.con I've heard of yet
I asked for a boy and they've sent me a girl,
That's the last time *I'll* buy on the internet

January 1, 8, 15, 22

When Gents of the Press with nowt better to do
Pondered together "Who next shall we screw?"
Poor old Mandy
Came in handy

I love little Bushy
His smile is so warm
But if we don't watch him
He'll do us great harm

A holocaust's poised over Israel,
Their new PM's fanning the flame
Sharon my daughter's so sickened
She's decided to change her name…

We seem to worship N.A.T.O.
Like our blesséd White Cliffs of Dover
When all it means, it seems to me,
Is North America Takes Over

January 29, February 5, 12, 19

Pity the desperate farmer
Battered from north to south
Kicked in the teeth by BSE
Then clobbered by foot and mouth

❖

Snow storms, rail horror, Foot & Mouth
Disasters piling high
The brain reels, one starts to feel
The End o' the World is Nigh…

❖

Now it's known that Mandy *didn't* lie
Will news hacks line up eating humble pie?
Apologies they'll write, with headlines high?
Well when they do, I'll know that pigs can fly

❖

"I've decided I *won't* fight pollution" says Bush
"My poll pledge? Shucks, guys – a … *mistake!*"
….How many more farts in the face of the globe
Must our "special relationship" take?

February 26, March 5, 12, 19

Dustman, Traffic Warden, Social Worker, Teacher –
We need our public servants, they're a necessary feature
Although we pay them peanuts, they deserve appreciation
So why do lotsa media folk dish out denigration?

❖

We *must* ensure our meat can be exported
So Foot & Mouth's the 'flu we fear and dread
But wait. We export – but we also *import!*
So why don't we just eat our own instead?

I've been spying on my Chinese neighbour
From the road outside his house most nights
But then I dropped my camera and he's kept it!
What's his *prob*lem? I *demand* my rights!

Vaccinate or exterminate?
The grim question faces the nation
Many farms plead "Let's *keep* our stock"
"Kill!" say others, " – and compensation!"

March 26, April 2, 9, 23

"Please – I'm a Kurd – flee Iraq – Saddam torture – "
"We're the Home Office, we don't *care* who caught yer!
Asylum? Forget it! Er ... Saddam's OK!!!
We'll say what suits us. You? On yer way!"

❖

Dear Tony, our back yard is *not* the right place
For Bush's mad Star Wars and crazed new arms race
If he's twisting your arm and you've got to save face
At least be straight with us. This is *our* space

❖

Twelve coppers, three cars, in case Ronnie Biggs
In his wheelchair attempts to fly
And 6,000 more to block May Day processions
"We need more Police!" cries the Met. Is that why?

I'd like to expose the private lives
Of Press men who spotlight their prey
But there's nought to expose, for newspaper owners
Don't ever sin. OK?

April 30, May 7, 14, 21

I'm a joiner, I sell my hands
I'm a doctor, I sell my brain
I'm a postman, I sell my feet
We're *all* prostitutes, ain't that plain?

❖

O Democracy! Is this thy sting
That the Parties are the same in almost everything
Yet if from the voting booth I grumpily defected
The *only-slightly-better* lot might not get elected?

Lifelong Labour but I almost abstained
And I wouldn't have felt ashamed
With most things, ok, they've fought some good fights
But they've really screwed up on our civil rights

Executed: Timothy McVeigh
The all-time worst terrorist in the USA –
Not counting, of course, the times
The US commits its own terrorist crimes

May 28, June 4, 11, 18

X-billion pounds from public funds
To fix the faults of Railtrack
But once they're back in profit again
Won't it be nice when they give us it back?

They killed poor Jamie Bulger
When they were kids aged ten
If we jailed them now for the rest of their lives
Would it bring Jamie back again?

"You *must* stop this Intifada!
"Palestinos, you *must* understand
"That it's simply God's Will," says Sharon
"That we build our settlements on your land"

❖

"The public *deserves* the best services!"
Ministerial speech-writers pen
But what if we can't all afford them?
Bet we won't all deserve the best then

June 25, July 2, 9, 16

There was an old lady who lived in a shoe
She had so many channels she didn't know what to do
By the time she'd read the listings to see what she could get
She'd no time left to watch the set

I took a little break, to get away from it all
Sheer bliss, change of scene, fresh air
But when I got back, would you believe it?
It was all still there

Oh Mr Trimble
What shall we Loyalists do?
The IRA's decommissioning
But we wanna believe it's not true

❖

Who lays down his life for his country
Is a hero. Top of the list.
Unless his country is somewhere else.
Then, he's a terrorist.

July 23, August 6, 13, 20

Maggie's been hitting the headlines again…
Remember her Thatcher Foundation?
We're still giving her sixty-thousand a year
Ask your MP about this donation

My secret for safer driving
Be you eight wheels, four wheels or chopper
Imagine the driver in front is a fool
And the driver behind is a copper

Top companies are folding so often these days
The news gets too painful to bear
Yet businessmen are what's needed, it's said,
To run public services. Oh yeah?

You *could* say the US got what they deserved
For the mayhem they've spread all these years
But their arrogant big boys who've trampled the globe
Aren't the poor sods now weeping the tears

August 27, September 3, 10, 17

A terrible tragedy struck America
We all share their grief at such mayhem
Yet few seem to know *why* their nation is hated…
And their media, it seems, never tells them

We, blinkered masses, don't know what to do
So we bay for blood, join the hullabaloo,
Of grown-up boys in SECURITY hats,
World follow-me Leaders, and smooth fat cats

Once we've killed Bin Laden
Though the price be World War Three
We can then get back to business –
There'll be no more terrorists, see?

Just at the moment, I've had enough war
It isn't the sole thing 4-liners are for
I wish I could think of some odd joke or foible
That might make us laugh and make life more enjoyble

September 24, October 1, 8, 15

You mustn't raise your voice
To suggest we haven't 'got it'
For to criticise in time of war
Isn't patriotic

Said Hitler "I wanted the world to hate Jews
"But how can I do it? I'm dead…
"I know! Re-incarnate as Ariel Sharon
"And get him to do it instead"

The 5th this year could mark a costly conflagration
For we've now declared ourselves the kind of nation
That, bombing and burning till we catch our Guy,
Forks out the costs till the day we die

Dearest child, here's today's lesson:
Violence has always begat
More of the same; so to teach you
it's wrong to hit others – take *that!*

October 22, 29, November 5, 12

We'll lock 'em up without a trial.
That's it. We will not funk it.
"Liberties? Airy fairy stuff!"
Quoth justice minister Blunkett

Said Major to Railtrack "Two thirds of this deal
"Will be subsidies – taxpayers' share"
"Gee thanks, John!" they chortled – yet still mucked it up
And shareholders weep "It ain't *fair!*"

When Afghanistan's flattened
And our boys get back
Hey, guys – what say?
Let's go bomb I-raq!

❖

I'm Murdoch, unelected, but I want your TV space
And I'm also 'gainst the Euro. So let's see…
Your British Government had better give me what I want
Or my Sun'll kick 'em out. Ya don't cross *me*

November 19, 25, December 3, 10

IF we can look away while bombers reign
IF we can watch kids starve and feel no pain
IF we think none but "terrorists" are to blame
Then great! We'll enjoy Christmas once again!

❖

If Santa turns up at your party
Check before starting the fun
Make sure that his beard's the right colour
'Cos he might be Bin L, on the run

❖

'Tis no longer wise old Santa
And just one sweet little fairy at
His Grotto. It's a cash crop now
And we're just a Lumpen Shoppertariat

December 17, 24, 31

2002

Afghan 'terrorists' locked up in Guantanamo Bay… US Govmnt budgets extra $45b for 'defence'… Spike Milligan dies… Sadam has masses of WMD (say Bush & Blair)… Million anti-war protesters march in London… Terror scare at Heathrow… Min of Health orders enough small-pox vaccine to immunise the whole nation… Queen Mum has 101st birthday – then dies… Minor earthquake in Manchester… Elections in France – Le Pen's party nearly wins… France lifts ban on British beef… Countryside Alliance spends £1m on London demo against fox-hunting… Myra Hindley dies… Cherie Blair conned … US places Star Wars nukes – near Harrogate…

On the 25th day of December
Was the wondrous message intoned
That to us was born, in Virginia,
Five little piglets, cloned

❖

India's planting minefields
'gainst Pakistan. Principle enshrined?
The old one – "What's your's is mine
"And what's mine is gonna be mined"

❖

"We'll chain you up in cages
"Furniture? Use jerrycans
"Human Rights? All that stuff?
"Ferget it," they said, "We're *Americans"*

❖

Please help us, World! cries Afghanistan
We're flattened, we're starved, we despair...
Wa-al, we've done *our* bit, says America
Gave you billions in bombs, ain't that fair?

January 7, 14, 21, 28

All around the countryside
The NFU's in panic
"They're going to cut our subsidies
"Unless we go organic!"

❖

Did Tony give Leo the jab?
If he did, will the outcome be fab?
Well yes, while sensational capers
Continue to sell lots of papers

❖

'Forty-five *billions* more on defence!'
Screams Herr Bush. It's crazy. It doesn't make sense.
The whole world quakes at this mad fool's earthshakers
Excepting, of course, US arms makers

❖

I used to ask for a tin of paint
Or a can … My problem's not drastic
But what on earth do we ask for,
Now the container is plastic?

February 4, 11, 18, 25

Alas, poor Spike, we've lost you
But now you're in Heaven above
We'll try to remember your teachings
Of marvellous humour – and love

They've got weapons of mass destruction?
Missiles? Chemicals? You bet – sure as hell!
Then it's right, we must take out Iraq. But
Does it follow we take out the US as well?

Big demo in London last week!
10,000, the marchers claimed, that night
Ah, *marchers* – they *always* claim high –
What? These were Policemen? … Oh… right…

One hundred and one and a bit
Not bad, when you think about it…
Part of our lives, for so many years…
We'll miss you, dear lady… Bon voyage… with tears

March 4, 11, 18, April 1

The Middle East conflict gets worse
The world waits in deathly hush
Will things really get better
Now that shove is coming from Bush?

❖

We DEMAND more cash for the NHS!
We DEMAND better deals for our troops!
We DEMAND more money for law and schools!
We DEMAND to pay more tax – oops …

❖

Time now that we Jews must ask ourselves
How long can this go on?
Are we still the Children of Israel
Or the Savages of Sharon?

❖

Many French didn't bother to vote
"Waste of time!" was the cry. But then
They realised, and so must we,
That le vote can be mightier than Le Pen

April 8, 15, 22, 29

You can keep your big store 'loyalty cards'
And other gimmicks spivvy
The best value's proved to be
The good old Co-op divi

You can't trust Politicians
They're all liars and you oughter
Rubbish everything they say.
Trust me: I'm a Reporter

"What fun!" giggles the Media
"Old Byers is *ever* so vexed!
"*We* rule without being elected!
"Now – who shall we kick out next?"

❖

We still love you, Queenie
So all the polls say
But you really must come clean
On all that loot you've stashed away…

May 20, 27, June 3, 10

Zooming along the motorway
Passing them all, keeping ahead
Wow! In another few seconds
I could be dead

❖

In the complex arena of politics
Who is honest we just have to guess –
The spin doctors of the Government?
Or the smear doctors of the Press?

❖

Bassam Saadi, young scamp, was up to his tricks
But life's tough, here on the West Bank
So we shot him, although he was aged only six –
He was throwing stones at our tank!

❖

Hand dryers in loos
Are all you can get
They warm your hands nicely
But still leave them wet

June 17, 24, July 1, 8

If we *must* sell "defence" to the Middle East
Why not sell anti-tank guns to Arafat?
His kids then could stop exploding themselves
While our arms firms could still keep on getting fat

❖

UK Coal says "We're closing Selby
"We're sorry but what can we do?
"What this country needs is more business parks
"So that's what we're building. Stuff you."

❖

I'm gonna crack down on those fraudsters
As your President I'm gonna hit back!
Wassat? – folks is askin' 'bout *my* deals?
… right … Declare war on Iraq.

❖

"Molesters!" screamed the lynch mobs,
Council, Press – "It's death they've earned!"
Eight years later, two child workers
Are proved guiltless. Have we learned?

July 15, 22, 29, August 5

They make weapons of mass destruction
They shun treaties all others obey
Their leader was only elected by fraud
So fair's fair, perhaps we should bomb USA?

❖

To prove things by statistics
This is all you need to know:
Decide what facts you're claiming
Then say "Here's what the figures show"

❖

If you think there's a paedophile living near you
Hunt him down, point the finger, you'll soon call his bluff
You're sure to be right, says the *News of the World*.
You made a mistake? Oh well, that's just tough

❖

Oh it's time that they brought back the birch
And the hangman, to protect you and I
Oh it's time we got back to those good old days
When no-one broke the law. And pigs used to fly.

August 12, 19, 26, September 2

One year on from September Eleven
Where is hope? The whole world has changed
We're all on the brink of war with Iraq –
Saddam the Wicked *v* Bush the Deranged…

The whole world, in this 'Fight Against Evil'
Could descend into ruin and mayhem…
Yet it isn't Americans who make me despair
It's the criminal loonies who lead 'em

Fox Hunt lobby spends a million pounds
London streets filled from morning till night
Unions, Peaceniks have known nothing like it
Oh, those poor landowners! Oh, pity their plight!

'Must have!' after *'Latest!'*
What will they sell us next?
I'm ancient. Can you tell me please
Why is it *Fantastic!* to send messages in 'text'?

September 9, 16, 23, 30

When 400-thou joined the 'Countryside' march
    Did the papers report it? Oh *yes!*
Then the Anti-war march, which was nearly as big
Wasn't mentioned. Rejoice! We have a free Press…

❖

Do like we tell yah, UN, says Bush
Then we'll say you're a world force for good
But if yah won't – hell, we'll do it ourselves!
Either way, *we're* the guys ruling this 'hood

❖

In Washington (Tyne & Wear) you can't
Have a demo. There's someone who says you shan't.
You see, the Town Centre is owned by the Pru'
And they say "Hop it!" to townsfolk like you

❖

I wouldn't like his job
And he has to pay the rent
But really, Mr Fireman –
Forty per cent?

October 7, 11, 21, 28

Hitler, claiming *'lebensraum'*, kicked off World War 2
And now another cauldron's on the boil
In the name of *'Anti-terror!'*, we're off to World War 3
So the US can take over Saddam's oil

❖

They're having staff problems at Buckingham Palace
The papers are leaping with gleeful malice
But what shall we do if we sack the Queen –
Elect as President some party has-been?

❖

North Yorks Moors folk – seems you've had it
Geof Hoon's about to let 'Star Wars' inhabit
If you don't want it he'll say "Well, tough
The Pentagon wants it so for me that's good enough"

❖

Suicide bombers strike again
And now an airliner near-shot from the sky
Yet still all we think of is "Catch 'em!" and "Kill 'em!"
O when will we pause, and ask ourselves *"Why?"*

November 11, 18, 25, December 2

Keep your eye on GATS
Their world-wide laws are looming
"Corporations shall rule" they say,
"All *you're* for is consuming…"

We don't like Tony Blair, or his wife
So we'll do our best to fix things so they fail.
We've the right to bring down Governments if we want to
'Cos we're owners of newspapers, like *The Scotsman*
and *The Mail*

If you go down Fylingdales today
You're in for a big surprise
The Yanks are fencing it off, they say
You'd better avert your eyes…

In holy halls on Christmas Day
We worship. Peace prevails.
In shopping malls on Boxing Day
We worship New Year Sales

December 9, 18, 23, 30

2003

The Northern Echo

Anti War Rally, children truant to join in… cloned sheep Dolly dies… Ken Livingstone's £5 congestion charge… Blix says Saddam has no WMD… Blair, Bush, insist we invade… Robin Cook resigns… March 20th – Invasion begins… April 14th – Bush says 'We won!'… Brown gives new mums £100 maternity benefit (for a year)… Clare Short resigns over war… BBC reporter Gilligan alleges sex-up…David Kelly suicide… Hutton Inquiry blames BBC… Lord Archer freed… Directory Enquiries closes… Aug. temp 100.6° – highest ever… Blunkett demands ID cards… President Bush in Sedgefield… Arnie Governor of California – without chads… Duncan-Smith ousted – Michael Howard lives again…

Floods and storms
Way past all norms
Surely, Mr President, this is global warming?
Naw… It's terrorists, like Ah keep warnin'

❖

From England to Venezuela
From Europe to Asia to Africa –
Peoples of the World, *Unite!*
We've nothing to lose but America

❖

We really must host the Olympics
T'will cost billions, but sport needs a boost in UK
It's a fact, we just don't hear sport mentioned
Except on TV. And mags. And the Press. Every day

❖

Oh Blunkett, Blunkett, whatever became
Of thee, once known to be so sane?
You now wipe civil liberties off your list
The minute anyone says 'terrorist'

January 6, 12, 20, 27

So many new reasons for war on Iraq
I can see now Saddam *must* be busted...
Then I think of regimes that the US *supports*
And I think... can these Bush men be *trusted*?

❖

We do take for granted the everyday things
So let's take a moment to offer up thanks
for the humbly labelled 'Doulton'. And 'Twyford'.
And let's not forget blessèd 'Armitage Shanks'

❖

Georgie Porgy sat on a bomb,
(cost $63 BILLION) to hurl down upon
Iraq. But promised, for those not slain,
$15 mil to put them together again

❖

I saw a nice car in an ad
But the ad said "No time wasters"
So I went and bought my car from someone else
'Cos who buys cars without tasters?

February 3, 10, 17, 24

Whatever is said by Mr Blix
The chorus will come "Saddam's up to his tricks!"
And tiniest nations will see right from wrong
When Bush diplomats sing the cheque-book song

❖

We lament "Youth don't care about politics
They just spend their time getting up to daft tricks"
Yet last week, when schoolkids demo'd against war
Some Heads were disgusted – "That's *not* what school's for!"

❖

Y'see, I *must* do what America wants.
You don't like it, I know. It's a hard one.
But if I refuse, the world will end up
... doing just what America wants ... (*er...pardon...?*)

❖

"Frenchies veto UN". Their 13th time!
(Well ok, we done hundred 'n' four)
But fellers – this Chirac's *unreasonable*
Chrissakes! All we *wanted* was war

March 3, 10, 17, 24

If you hated the guts of our Government
(Unlikely, I know…); but if true
Would you want those American bombers
To come and liberate you?

❖

England *v* Turkey, international match
At Sunderland's Stadium of Light
"Let's show we're a great sporting nation, lads –
Get drunk, grab bricks, an' let's have a fight!"

❖

We can bomb everybody to peace
(give or take some "co-lateral" pieces…)
But we now find restoring order
Is somewhat harder…

❖

If we think some guys are terrorists, even kids, we say
Lock 'em up without a trial, in Guantanamo Bay
So thank us, you Iraquis, after all your years of strife
That we're bringing you democracy, *our* way of life

March 31, April 7, 14, 28

We'll run your schools and your hospitals
We welcome your Finance Initiative
We pick off the cherries then you'll pay our debts.
That's business. We take, we don't give

When my Dad bought a suit, he bought it for life
It was 'Best', and he kept it for trips with t' wife
But my kids won't be seen dead in clothes bought last week
For fear that their mates will think them a freak

The Blairs and the Bushies went out to play
"Let's have a war! I know! Let's say –
"*Saddam has bombs! We're gonna be nuked!*"
Seems now Saddam hadn't. Guess we've been duped…

❖

Conrad Black, Rupert Murdoch and Lord Rothermere
Dictate what we think, that's perfectly clear.
Whatever the Government might actually say
They'll twist it, and feed us half-truths, every day

May 5, 12, 19, 26

'He's got WMD's *now!* We *must* go to war!'
So we went. But now we wonder – what *was* it for?
The warnings, it seems, were less than truthful
No wonder Tony now is looking less than youthful

❖

If we all switched our tellies off 'stand-by'
We could save £40 millions a year
Besides which, we'd know we were doing our bit
To help stop polluting the atmosphere

❖

Welcome home Alan, Darlington's son
We suspect you of nothing that's sinister
The fact is we realise it's far from fun
Living the life of a Minister

❖

Grow your food farmer then gather your seeds
To plant them for next year's crop –
Unless, that is, you've switched to GM
In which case, you can't. Your freedom's been stopped

June 2, 9, 16, 23

Pensioner! Take a careful look
As the Ministry dumps the Pension Book.
Choose 'Post Office Card Account'. It's a must
Or your local Post Office could go bust

❖

Folk who get their fun by killing foxes
Show taste, in my view, somewhat un-sublime
But face it, nature's animals all die that way,
And really, was it worth all that precious MP time?

❖

They're "trying" two Brits in Guantano' Bay
So come on Tony – what do you say?
Enough of the diplomat's whispering shop
Shout at Bush – "THIS HAS GOT TO STOP!"

❖

"I sincerely believed what I told you was true"
Well I'm sure that you did, dear Tone
But 'sincere' – well, Maggie – and Hitler – had that …
Sincere's not enough on its own

June 30, July 7, 14, 21

The BBC has always been
A target for Governments, old and new
Which probably shows the Beeb's about right
In playing it straight for me and you

❖

In the minds of Government
And the market's manic voices
We're not humans, we're 'consumers'
And all we need is 'choices'

❖

Global warming, climate change
News of disasters every day
The answer? Bury your head in the sand
Then it'll go away

❖

Oil's been discovered in Wiltshire!
Well watch out. Although it sounds strange
Wilts County Council had better prepare –
The Pentagon's bound to want regime change

July 28, August 4, 11, 18

Lord Hutton's sensational findings
Won't bring Dr Kelly back
In the end, he was just one more victim
Of that justified... necessary... vital...
peace-ensuring... liberating...
totally humanitarian...
War on Iraq

❖

The operator on 192
Would give you the number and that's all you do
But it's 118 now, then a daft numbers dance
And will it be cheaper? Fat chance!

❖

We're sending costly satellites to Mars
To see if there is life on that red turf
If there is, we'll probably just kill it
The way we do with life here on earth

August 25, September 1, 8

We got thirteen rotting warships, polluting Pennsylvania
We got problems. This ain't cool
Well we ain't gonna break 'em in the U.S. of A.
We'll send the crap across the pond, to Hartlepool

❖

Retail therapy is good for you!
Stores and HP companies show you how
To fill your house with expensive junk
And then go bankrupt. Feel better now?

❖

So sorry, little girl, for bulldozing Mummy's house
But she knew that living there would really nettle us
She built her house on what we say should be Israeli land
And we're here to guard our brave illegal settlers

❖

Iraq's too damn' costly. Whatever we do
Along comes some guy in a terrorist hat
They're even destroying the oil we came here for
Shucks! Who'd a' thought they'd do *that?*

September 15, 22, 29, October 6

I'm Arnold Schwarzenegger
Don't mess with me – I'm mega!
Now I'm boss of California
I jest thought I'd better warn ya

If a man says he *knows* God's will
'Cos he saw it in his bible
Is he fundamentally honest?
Or fundamentally tribal?

Oh naughty Georgie Galloway
The Party was shocked to hear you say
To our troops that it would be illegal to fight
When your Leader *sincerely* had said it was right

❖

The fate of poor Mr Duncan-Smith
Is bound to make one think "What if…?"
Take care, Tony, though your sky is blue
That such a fate isn't waiting for you

October 13, 20, 27, November 3

You've invited George Bush to State Visit?
Oh, Tone – that's not sensible, is it?
He's the moron who led you astray!
Tell him you've cancelled, send him away

"I'll insist you must all have ID cards"
Said Blunkett. And that's what he did
"And when they are ready," he says,
"You'll all have to buy one. At seventy-odd quid"

If you claim you're inspired by religion
Reason don't matter a smidgeon
For example, that's why al Quaeda
Can rejoice when they kill some poor bleeder

❖

We know how to handle protestors
While telling the world 'We have freedom!'
'Protect' them behind Police cordons
So the rest of the world won't see them

November 10, 17, 24, December 1

When I needed to go to hospital
They looked after me very well
So why, when quizzed by a pollster
Did I say "NHS? It's *hell!*" ?

Our kids need safety systems
That work in *every* case
It would be simple really
If we weren't the human race

On the 13th day of Christmas my true love said to me
'Enough now, of shopping till we drop!'
We gathered all the presents that we really didn't want
And we took them to the Oxfam shop

December 15, 22, 29

2004

(The story so far...)
Madrid train station bombed...
US Presidential Election year...
World News: Becks unfaithful to
Posh... Israeli whistle-blower
Vanunu released after 18 years...
Iraqi prisoners tortured by US...
asylum seekers attacked...
Kerry stands against Bush...
Maxine Carr demonised....
UK becomes an obese zone...and
a Stakeholder Society...Israeli
whistleblower released...the *real*
Weapon of Mass Destruction...

The World According to Walinets

Great news! We had a great Christmas!
Great presents! The food was just great!
We're off to a great foreign holiday now
Away from that G word – it's starting to grate…

They kicked down my door at four a.m.
And arrested me. Think of the shame…
"You must be a terrorist," they said
"You've got an unusual name"

The day to re-elect me
Is comin' mighty soon
So don't think about I-raq –
We're gonna colonise the Moon!

❖

TV documentaries now
Seem to think we're thick
And need, to grasp the simplest point –
Crash! Bang! Music!

January 5, 12, 19, 26

Hutton says the Government's won.
Some say he felt he must…
They now fear Tone will take revenge
And the Beeb will bite the dust…

No parole for Maxine Carr
Blunkett thinks it's best by far
To change the law. He's now a hearty
Member of the Lynch Mob Party

Let us build you a brand new supermart!
Forget all those shopkeepers' sighs
You can all save yourselves lots of pennies
While around you your town just dies…

Innocent (13) said "My Dad
"Was strangled last night, then Mum was burned.
"I'd like to apply for asylum
"Do you think my request will be spurned?"

February 2, 16, 23, March 1

We've got your release from Guantanamo!
You can come home at last and be free
Or – maybe we'll lock you in Belmarsh,
And throw away the key…

I think 9/11. I think Madrid.
And of everything else that terrorists did…
What is it we're doing, so terribly remiss,
That provokes so many to act like this?

Who would a politician be
To deal with folks like you and me?
You want *this* and I want *that*
And both of us want it in ten minutes flat

❖

I used to be a citizen
Humble, nothing bolder
But glory be, congratulate me
For now – I'm a Stakeholder!

March 8, 15, 22, 29

For the next Presidential election
Kerry's raised 20mil bucks, they say…
But Bush has raised more than 150…
Dollarmocracy rules, OK!

❖

From Iraq the news is horrific
God knows what can happen next
Yet the tabloid front pages are filled
With the latest on Posh and Becks…

❖

You don't want foreigners killed?
You don't like to see civil liberties chilled?
You reckon regime change by bombing is terrible?
You must be a woolly, a lefty, a liberal

❖

Israel in secret made nukes by the dozen
Then Vanunu spilled the beans
So they threw him in jail for eighteen years
Claiming that's what "freedom" means

April 5, 12, 19, 26

I went to a funeral last week
One person dead – hundreds tearful and sad…
How I weep for those thousands who now in Iraq
Mourn a loved one..or a soldier..Oh Bush – are you *mad?*

❖

This terrible news on interrogants
We sure agree with the clamourers
Our Pentagon guys can do without this –
We're gonna forbid all cameras

❖

So many issues the tabloids could chase,
Things more important by far
But no, they scream to self-righteous hooligans
"Let's get Maxine Carr!"

❖

There's a weapon of mass destruction,
Biological, lethal in every way
Huge power, it threatens the whole of the world
Its name is the U S of A…

May 3, 10, 17, 24

Oh *do* buy our chockies and burgers
They're ever so good for our wealth
Ignore these Government spoilsports
With their "Eating can damage your health"

❖

As oil prices hit the roof
Oil company cash tills ring...
One wonders – are we getting the truth?
Oh! How could I *say* such a thing?

❖

Well, there's your lesson, Tony
Let's hope you can hear it
If not, next year the Tories are back
And I don't think we could bear it...

❖

YouGov, the pollsters, tell the Press
What we, the people, are saying -
That is, the people on the internet -
You others aren't worth surveying

May 31, June7, 14, 21